Going to the Doctor

A TODDLER PREP™ BOOK

About Toddler Prep™ Books

The best way to prepare a child for any new experience is to help them understand what to expect beforehand, according to experts. And while cute illustrations and fictional dialogue might be entertaining, little ones need a more realistic representation to fully understand and prepare for new experiences.

With Toddler Prep™ Books, a series by ReadySetPrep™, you can help your child make a clear connection between expectation and reality for all of life's exciting new firsts. Born from firsthand experience and based on research from leading developmental psychologists, the series was created by Amy and Aaron Pittman – parents of two who know (all too well) the value of preparation for toddlers.

We're going to the doctor! It's important to go to the doctor because they help our bodies stay healthy and strong.

There will be so many new things to see and do. Let's talk about what happens when we go to the doctor.

When we get to the doctor's office we go to the front desk to check in.

Then, we sit and wait for our turn. There are lots of chairs inside the waiting room.

Sometimes, the waiting room has books and toys. You might see other kids waiting for the doctor, too.

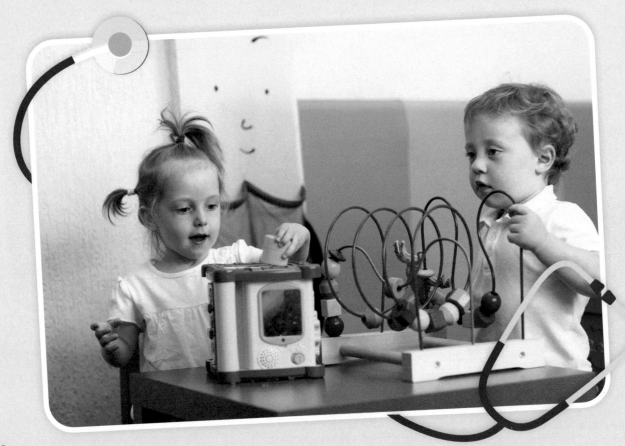

When it's our turn, the nurse calls your name and takes us to the back. The nurse is the doctor's helper.

Before we see the doctor, the nurse checks to see how much you've grown. First, you stand on a scale to see how heavy you are.

Then, you stand next to a big ruler to see how tall you are.

Next, we go into the exam room. Inside there is a table to sit on and tools for the doctor to use.

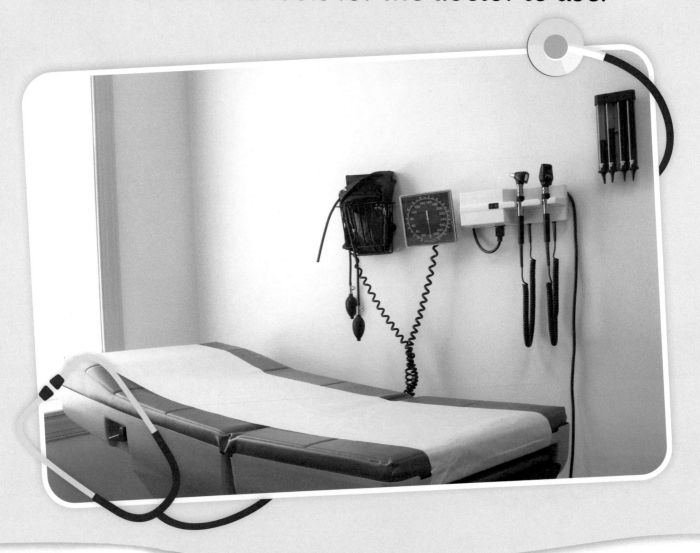

The nurse uses a tool called a thermometer to take your temperature.

Sometimes when we go to the doctor, you need to get a shot to stay healthy. Shots feel like a pinch and can hurt a little, but not for long.

When you get a shot, the nurse cleans the spot with a small wipe that smells funny.

Then, it's time for the shot. It's ok if you feel a little scared. You can hug your stuffed animal or look at me.

Finally, the nurse puts a fun bandage on the spot where you got your shot.

After the nurse leaves, we wait patiently for the doctor. We can read books or play with toys while we wait.

We might need to take off your clothes so the doctor can see how strong your body is.

When the doctor comes in, they ask some questions about how you have been feeling.

Next, the doctor uses a stethoscope to listen to your heart go, "ba-bum, ba-bum, ba-bum."

After the doctor listens to your heart, they use an otoscope to look in your ears. It doesn't hurt, but it might tickle - try not to wiggle!

Then, the doctor looks inside your nose and mouth. Open wide and say "AH!"

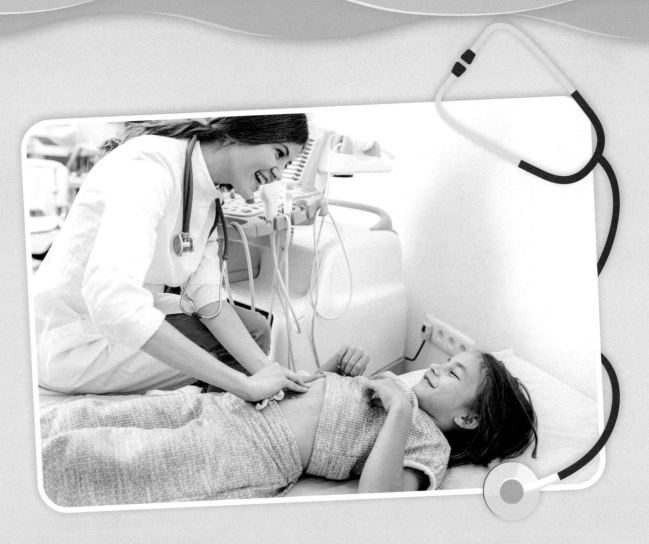

Finally, the doctor might press on your tummy and check other parts of your body to make sure everything is ok.

Hooray! You did it! Time to pick a sticker and say goodbye until next time.

Made in United States
Troutdale, OR
03/07/2024

18260299R00017